From Boy

To

Ol' Chap

A story & history

of

Tiddington

Oxon

http://www.fast-print.net/bookshop

FROM BOY CHAP TO OL' CHAP
Copyright © Ian Morris 2015

ISBN 978-178456-246-5

First Published 2015 by
Fast-Print Publishing of Peterborough, England.

A message from the author

Some ten(ish) years ago, I decided to write a history of the village for two young members of the cricket club; subsequently a third member joined the triumvirate.

These three young people graduated from primary to secondary school, where they were required to do a project about their own village, including economic and historical aspects.

I'm pleased to say that one of the three received top marks. Mission accomplished!

My history project then went to sleep until a local farmer had some relations over here from Canada. I had to truncate some of the aspects of the history for this volume. The two Canadian bears came, stayed and then went on the 27th of June 2015; their visitation provoked me into finishing the project.

Ian Morris

Acknowledgements

The Blacksmith's Daughter

The Licensed Victualler's Daughter

The Motor Mechanic's Daughter

The Lady and Gentleman in the Big House

Mrs K Lawton

And also the good folk of Aldberie and Titendone (the old names for Aldbury and Tiddington).

Drawings for the map by Lucy and Ickford Primary School 'Young Uns'.

This is a tribute to Kenny the Clock.
Ken Lawton was a much loved character in this village.
He assisted in the design of this book.

Preface

This is a story about a young Oxfordshire lad's passage through life as told by history, starting with the Iron Age and finishing with the Great War, as an Ol' Chap.

It is also about the small hamlet of Tiddington – about eight miles from Oxford – where the author was born and has lived all of his life.

"AND I SAW ANOTHER ANGEL FLY IN THE MIDST OF HEAVEN, HAVING THE EVERLASTING GOSPEL TO PREACH UNTO THEM THAT DWELL ON THE EARTH, AND TO EVERY NATION, AND KINDRED, AND TONGUE, AND PEOPLE, SAYING WITH A LOUD VOICE, FEAR GOD, AND GIVE GLORY TO HIM; FOR THE HOUR OF HIS JUDGMENT IS COME; AND WORSHIP HIM THAT MADE HEAVEN, AND EARTH, AND THE SEA, AND THE FOUNTAINS OF WATERS."—REVELATION XIV. 6, 7.

"In the beginning God created the heavens and the earth..."

...the light

...the firmament

... the separation of the waters

...the sun, the moon and the stars

...man in the image of God

and also the appointment of food.

Jack Pike

Greater Spotted Newt

The Devil
(Oxford)

Highway man under the Moon

Highwayman caught an punished for

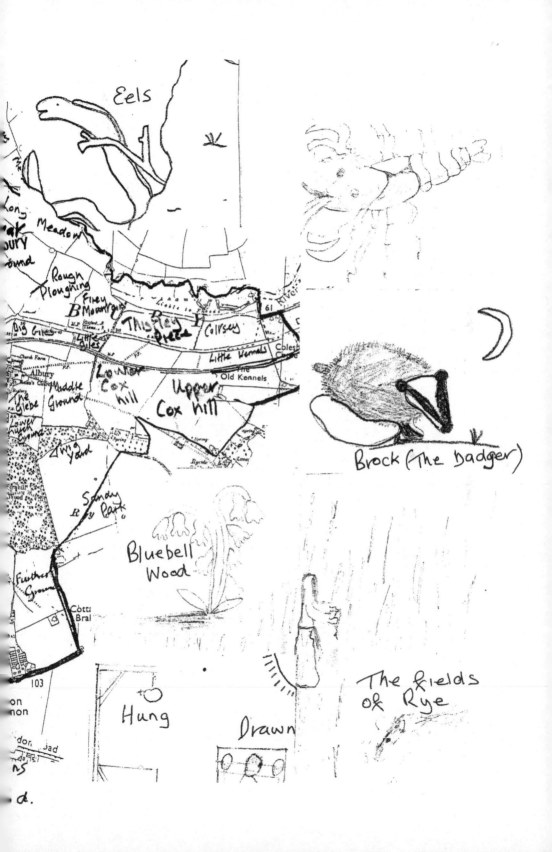

Eels

Brock (The Badger)

Bluebell Wood

Hung

Drawn

The fields of Rye

The hamlet of Tiddington (Titendone) is born.

Prehistoric Titendone dates back into the sands of time. With the onset of the Bronze Age came the Beaker people, who were instrumental in a pastoral pattern of agriculture. They made their own woollen garments and pottery. The first wells would have been dug, and the well of the south side of the hill was probably one of the first. Also alcoholic drinks – honey based mead – were introduced to the hamlet and it has never been the same since!

The Iron Age

The Iron Age engulfed Titendone from about 800BC and continued until the Roman invasion. Some remains from that period have been found locally.

Emperor Claudius invaded at Richborough, Kent in AD43. It is believed that only four legions – Legio II Augusta, Legio IX Hispana, Legio XIV Gemina and Legio XX Valeria Victrix – were involved, totalling 20,000 men with roughly the same amount of auxiliaries.

Sometime between AD44-47, southern 'Brittaniae', including Titendone, was occupied.

Local Roman remains include a building and drain at the Three Pigeons, on Harrington Common, iron workings out on Camp Common ground and a forge and furnace at Camp Corner.

A well was probably sited on the south side of Tytta's hill and an encampment and temple at Isurium. Also, a minor road ran from Dorchester-upon-Thames to Fleet Marston, a civil parish and deserted medieval village near Aylesbury, about 30 miles west of St Albans.

Betwixt Cilworth Farm and Sandy Lane, the course of the Roman road is marked for nearly a mile, running just west of Trindal's Farm and Lower Farm. On a similar alignment, a footpath leads from Tiddington School to Albury. Then it takes the road down the hill at Albury to strike the modern road (A418) 300 yards east of the sharp bend by the benchmark 214.62 .

On the north side of the A418, a hedgerow in the field (known as Firery Mountain thus named after a Roman god), continues to line up over a slight ridge and for 200 yards, it coincides with the remains of an agger* in which the gravel metalling is visible (SP 658054). The same hedgerow has a kink at the top of the ridge and here the Roman road takes a slight realignment to run a few yards east without trace. Unfortunately the approaches to the Roman ford are not clearly defined, however, they are likely to be associated with the stepping stones past Camp Corner, crossing the cart way behind Holly Cottage over the Thame River at the stepping stones.

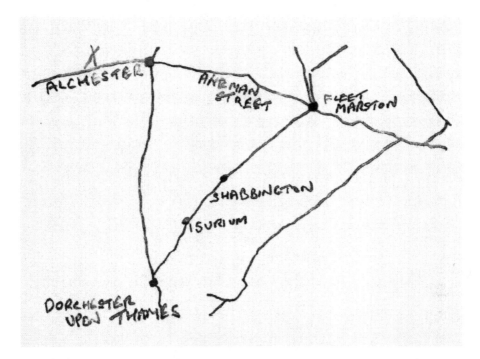

* The agger is built up foundations (under the surface cobbles) of a Roman road, the remains of which are sometimes found as a long earth bank.

In around AD410 the Romans went back whence they had come. Vortigern, king of the Britons, invited the Saxons to defend his Lordship. Vortigern himself assumed power within his homeland, presumed to be in Powys

Nuzzling in the knee of Tytta's Hill, lies the hamlet of Titendone: bordered by the Bucks Boys in the north, the Three Pigeons in the south, Colesheath Coppice in the east and by Morris's Spinney in the west.

In about AD635, Rome sent Birinus to convert the Pagans to Christianity. He was given the old town of Dorchester-upon-Thames. Aldbury is rumoured to be the temple site of Isurium and home of the second oldest Christian site in Oxfordshire, which was situated on the south side of what is now the churchyard. The presence of a Yew tree on the south side of God's acre has led to rumours that it could be a Saxon church.

Around this time the Church of Saint Helen, Tiddington-with-Albury was probably first built.

The original church at Alberie, which was dedicated to St Helen, was built in Saxon times.

It is said that Helen, after whom the church is named, became a saint after she went on a pilgrimage to Syria Palaestina, a Roman province. There, rumour has it, she discovered the True Cross – that being wood from the original cross on which Jesus was crucified.

Emperor Constantinus, governor of York, fell in love with the beautiful Helen, (daughter of Coel of Colchester). She gave birth to the emperor to be known as Constantine the Great.

The causeway on the way to Brohull (Brill) takes you into Mercia proper. At Yttingaford is the site of a treaty betwixt Alfred and the men with horns. Cometh AD1035, Cnut passed away and the next seven years were a time of great turmoil. Edward the Confessor, himself of Islip, became Lord King and the lands returned to much prosperity. In 1066, Alwig the Sheriff held

Titendone for Edward with a tithe of 30 shillings. Edward passed away in the winter of 1066 and Harold seized the Kingdom.

At Stamford Bridge, Harold fought Hardrada of Norway, won and thus had to march south to engage William the Conqueror at the Battle of Hastings. Harold was the last Saxon king.

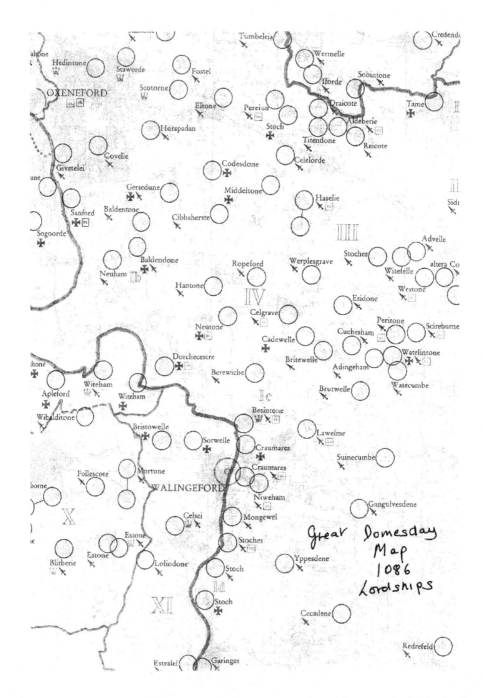

Great Domesday Map 1086 Lordships

Alecto (Domesday) Limited

Part Two

William was crowned at Westminster on Christmas Day in 1066.

The great Domesday book tells us that Alwig now held Titendone for King William. The manor consisted of '2 hides (a hide is 120 acres) and 3 virgates (each approximately 30 acres). He had some fields fallow and he had 'bordar' (low status serfs) to help. There were 15 acres of meadow. Tre now worth 40 shillings.'

Tre, in Saxon times, was the value of the whole of the estate.

Folklore

Plough Monday started the year being the first Monday after the 12 days of Christmas have passed.

Candlemas Day was the 2nd February

If it thunders in February then it will frost in April.

If February give much snow
A fine summer it doth foreshow,
The snowdrop, in purest white array,
First rears her head on Candlemas Day.

May Day celebrations took place from the 15th century. "There in Totendone are 2 'obby oss's, the ol' oss and the blue ribbon oss. There's not a budding boy or gal this day, but is got up and gone to bring in May."

Select four feathers
One of the Kite
One of the Swan
One of the Goose
And one of the Mallon
Temper them, silver sand
Cut into 4 sizes and then begin

This was the procedure for a 14th century monk to prepare a selection of quills.

In 1348 the Black Death came to Titendone. What was left of the folk from Aldberie migrated to Titendone.

In 1377, Joan Russell held the manor and married Thomas Quartremain of Reicote.

Their son Richard Quartremain became the Lord of Four Manors in 1398: Reicote, Aldberie, Titendone and Iford (Ickford).

The tax assessment for Titendone in 1415 was recorded as £1-16s-4d.

Richard passed away in 1477 and the manor went to Thomas Danvers, who was also the Lord at Wradenstok (Waterstock).

In 1483 the Wixon family had oxen out on Cilworth Common.

In 1502 Thomas passed away, and the manor wass left to Sybil, the wife.

In 1511 Sybil passed away and Elizabeth Cave inherited the manor. Lay subsidy was due; the first payment was 10s 8d and the second payment was 11s 6d, due in 1523.

By 1524, in Titendone, there were at least nine households: seven in service and two in wages. Three persons were taxed £8 worth of goods.

By 1526 the rector received £6-13s-4d in tithes, of which he paid his curate £4.

In 1530 Edward Cave inherited the manor.

The tithe value had risen to £9-2s-8d.

In 1539 the following men were called to muster roll for the Mary Rose. Bartyllmew Colles, Gabryell Baker, Robert Wyxton and James Wyxton were furnished with harness, billhook, sword and dagger. John Mynge, Roger Coles, Hugh Coles, Nicholas Perker and Richard Wyxton, had a billhook, bow and arrow, and sword and dagger.

The Highways Act of 1555 obliged each adult of each parish to give 6 days per annum to maintain the King's highway.

In 1566 Edward Cave passed away and the manor was administered by his wife Elizabeth.

In 1574 the manor changed ownership to Ann Rowles and John Hall.

1n 1592 Sir William Cave disputed the ownership of the manor in court. And lost!

Richard Wixon's wife passed away in 1598 and he then married Katherine Lankit.

Part Three

In 1606 John Hall sold the manor to Robert Waller.

Richard Wixon passed away in 1618, and his second wife Katherine passed away in 1629.

Edmund Waller, poet who supported the royalist cause, inherited the manor in 1620. Waller plotted against Parliament and in 1643 Edmund Waller was charged and convicted of 'displaying a very polforoorey'. He confessed whatever he had said, thought or had seen, and knew or suspected of others. For this his life was spared.

Waller was committed to the Tower of London, fined £10,000 (£3m in today's money) and banished from the realm.

Subsequently funds were raised to pay Edmund Waller's fine and he was released from the Tower. He took up residence in Rouen, France, with his second wife, Mary Bracey of Thame.

At the closure of Parliament in 1651, his sentence was revoked and he was allowed to return to England.

In 1636 the Reverend Samuel Keme became the rector of Oldbury commonly called Aldberie. Born, according to Matricula (the church register), in the City of London, he was educated at Magdalen Hall and later at Magdalen College.

He obtained the title of "the most notorious liar that ever wore long ears", the nickname given to him by his peers.

At the turn of times in 1641, he put a curate into his living and sided with the rebels. He took covenant and was made chaplain to and captain of a troop of horses in the regiment of Basil, Earl of Denbigh. He prayed and preached, often to encourage the soldiers to fight. He preached against the king and his followers. He endeavoured to make the soldiers believe that the king and all those about him were papists – or at least popishly affected.

However, in spite of all this, what is said of him paints a very different picture. He was reputed to be of a servile spirit, an epicure, a flatterer, a lecher and a knight of the post, who was a pretender to saintship. He certainly liked the ladies as he had four wives: Anne, Jemina, Mary and 'the buxom' Elizabeth.

Even his friends were a less-than-saintly bunch. One Thomas Vaughan, related to Henry Vaughan, alchemist and friend, died at Oldbury as a result of mercury sniffing.

At the Restoration again he saw his best chance and expressed his loyalty to King Charles II. As a result, he was allowed to keep his living at Oldbury. He passed away 10 years later.

In 1653 Richard Wixon sold his property to Simon Broadwater.

Bargain and sale.

Party 1: Richard Wixon of Titendone, yeoman farmer.

Party 2: Simon Broadwater and wife Elizabeth. University cook, residing in Oxford.

Party 1 grants party 2 his messuage and grounds. £400.

Witnesses:

Sampson Rawlins, William Wixon, Ralph Ingram and John Hopkins. August 1653

In 1661 William Wixon was obliged to mortgage his property for £150 to Robert Say, Provost of Oriel College, Oxford.

In 1664, the Hearth Tax of 1662, was raised from Thomas Coxhead, Widow Cowper, and William Wixon.

In 1665, Tithingtowne had seven households listed for Hearth Tax but only two had hearths.

On the 25th of March 1670, Bargain and Sale between Anne Wixon, widow, and William Wixon, cooper, a newly erected cottage, with three acres of pasture in "the Home Close" between the land of Thomas Coxhead (south) and Tiddington Straet (west). 1 pays 2 £100. Signed by the mark of 1. Witnesses - Jonas Chirch, Timothy Lewes, mark of Richard Wixon and Fish Lyne. 26th March 1670. PMB/G/12/7/6 (Pembroke College reference number).

The Compton Census of 1676 recorded 50 conformants over 16.

In 1685, the rectory was awarded two closes, north of Fernhill (Bluebell Wood) in lieu of land lost in the enclosure acts.

In 1688, Thomas Tatham settled in the cottage next to the old post office.

Various families were recorded at St. Helens during the 17th century: Wixons, Coxheads, Slaughters, Johnsons, Cowpers, Tatums and Tathams.

Part Four

On the 4th August in 1914, Great Britain declared war on Germany. The Lion versus the Eagle.

The old pals from Tiddington took the carrier's cart to St Giles and took the King's Shilling.

The next year compulsory conscription was introduced for fit men between 18 and 41 years. This meant that women went to work in ammunitions factories, as clippies on the buses or working on the land. Farming was hard work for the women as not only had the men gone to fight but many of the farm horses were requisitioned for war too.

Parliament passed laws banning bonfires and trespassing on other people's allotments. Food was needed to be sent to the soldiers fighting abroad so rationing was introduced.

By 1918 conscription went up to include those up to 51 years old.

On the 11th day of the 11th month of 1918 the war was over. Villagers returned home with various injuries. Six were never to return. A stained glass window depicting the Agony of Gethsemane was fitted in St Helen's in memory of those who lost their lives.

The Great War changed England for good. Women wore shorter skirts, dispensed with chaperons and smoked in public.

The hamlet was now entering the Depression.

- - - - - - - - -

1935

TO THE CHILDREN

A MESSAGE SENT TO THE CHILDREN BY HIS LATE MAJESTY KING GEORGE V ON THE OCCASION OF THE 25TH ANNIVERSARY OF HIS ACCESSION TO THE THRONE.

You are the heirs of a great past; but the future is yours, and is your high responsibility. Each of you must try to be a good citizen in a good city. To this end, you must make the best of all your powers. Strive to grow in strength, in knowledge, and in grace. If you persist bravely in this endeavour you will work worthily for your family, your city, your country, and for mankind. So to live, in whatever sphere, must be noble and may be great. My confident trust is in you.

GEORGE R.I.

Quotation taken from page 256 of *Seventy Glorious Years* (Oldham Press. 1937).

Thame Town Council   1st July 2007.
Town Hall
High Street
THAME.
Oxfordshire
OX9 3DP

Dear Sirs, I have read the latest issue No 4 of your journal "Thame Town Crier" with great interest and would make the following comment—

On the back page 8 you show an illustration of a man purporting to be planting decorative flowers.

The man depicted is, I believe, a certain Mr Jesse Matthews who, although appearing to be assiduous in his labours is giving a false picture.

He is, in fact, searching for a penny which he lost 5 or 6 years ago and for which he has been looking for ever since on the pretext of working

I must now confess that I picked up his penny an instant after he dropped it and having seen him spend hours, days, weeks, months and years — often in his own free time seeking in vain, I now return it herewith.

Would you, please, give it to him with my apologies. Stress to him the importance of declaring this extra income in his Income Returns to our new Darling Tax Collector.

        Yours very truly
           A Thame Citizen Wellwisher.

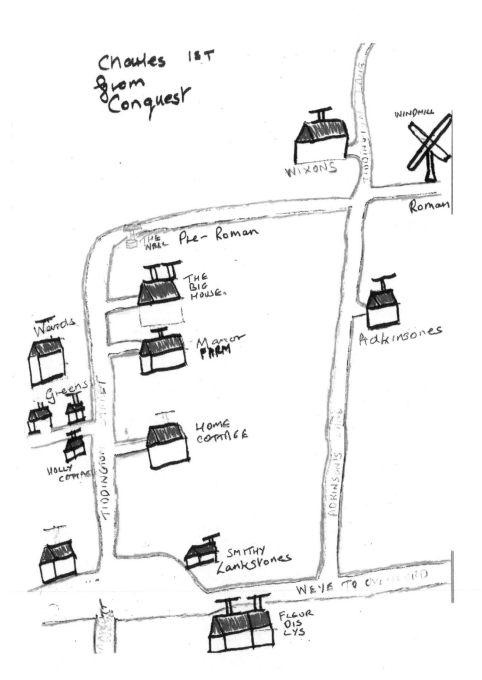

Charles 1st
from
Conquest

WINDMILL

WIXONS

Roman

THE WELL Pre-Roman

THE BIG HOUSE.

Wards

Manor FARM

Adkinsones

Greens

HOME COTTAGE

HOLLY COTTAGE

SMITHY
Lankstones

WE'YE TO OXE BED

FLEUR DIS LYS

The old chap sayeth

they sparrers as
ett all my pays,
best kivver they
up afor they
be gone

References

1   Three Pigeons ADS 47 AD
2   Roman Road 150AD Viatores
3   Isutium Station 625AD Dr Plot
4   Alfred Lord King of Wessex 878AD
5   St Helens Church 1180 Oxford Feet of Fines
6   Domesday 1086 Titendone
    2 Hides 3 Virgates
7   Muster Roll 1539 Bullingdon Hundred
    E36/28 Tydlington
8   Edward Cave 1530
9   Pembroke college 1653 Bargain & Sale, Messuage and Ground
10
11 Compton Census 1676
12 St Helens 1686 Belles, Richard Keane
13 2nd Oxford and Bucks, Nonne Bosschen defeating the Prussian Guard 1914 by W.B. Wollen
14 13th/14th Century budding boy or gal
15 Plough Monday – Ist Monday after the 12 days of Christmas
16 Candlemas, feast day
17 Ancient Well, Mark Robins 1988
18 The Bible, Genesis